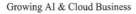

GROWING AI & CLOUD BUSINESS
High Impact Marketing

Abstract

"Growing AI & Cloud Business" offers strategic insights into leveraging marketing techniques to drive growth in AI and cloud sectors.

Mangesh Prabhavalkar
Email: mangeshap@gmail.com

Mangesh Prabhavalkar

grow
AI & Cloud
business

vol.1

High-Impact Marketing

Index

Chapter 1 Introduction to High-Impact Marketing

Overview

Welcome to "High-Impact Marketing: Growing Your AI and Cloud Consulting Firm." This eBook is designed to be your comprehensive guide to leveraging social media ads to achieve remarkable growth for your AI and cloud consulting firm. Whether you are just starting to explore digital marketing or looking to refine your existing strategies, this eBook will provide you with actionable insights and practical steps to make social media ads a powerful tool in your marketing arsenal.

The Power of Digital Marketing

In today's digitally connected world, traditional marketing methods alone no longer suffice. The shift to digital has transformed how businesses reach their target audiences. For AI and cloud consulting firms like yours, the potential of digital marketing is immense. Digital platforms allow you to target specific with precision, engage with them through personalized, and track the effectiveness of your campaigns in real time.

Social media, with its vast user base and sophisticated advertising tools, stands out as one of the most effective platforms for digital marketing. As of 2024, social media boasts over 2.9 billion monthly active users, making it a fertile ground for reaching potential clients across various industries. The platform's advanced targeting options, robust analytics, and diverse ad formats make it an ideal choice for consulting firms looking to expand their reach and drive growth.

Why AI and Cloud Consulting Firms Need Robust Digital Marketing

AI and cloud consulting firms operate in a highly competitive and rapidly evolving market. As businesses increasingly adopt digital transformation, the demand for AI and cloud solutions is soaring. However, this also means more players are entering the field, making it crucial for your firm to stand out. Robust digital marketing can help you:

Increase Brand Awareness: Establish your firm as a thought leader in the AI and cloud space. By sharing insights and success stories, you can build a strong brand presence.

Generate Quality Leads: Use targeted ads to reach decision-makers and IT leaders who are actively seeking AI and cloud solutions.

Enhance Customer Engagement: Engage with your audience through personalized content, addressing their specific pain points and highlighting how your solutions can benefit them.

Drive Conversions: Convert leads into clients by guiding them through a well-planned sales funnel, from awareness to decision-making.

Success Stories: Digital Marketing in Action

Consider the success story of a mid-sized cloud consulting firm, CloudTech Solutions, which managed to triple its client base within a year using social media ads. By creating targeted campaigns that showcased their expertise in cloud migration and security, they reached CIOs and CTOs of mid-sized companies who were looking for reliable partners to manage their digital transformation. Their ads included video testimonials, case studies, and educational content, which not only built trust but also demonstrated their value proposition effectively.

Another example is AI Innovators, an AI consulting firm that used social media ads to highlight their custom AI solutions for the healthcare industry. By focusing on specific pain points such as patient data management and predictive analytics, they attracted the attention of hospital administrators and healthcare IT managers. Their ad campaigns featured success stories from previous clients, interactive webinars, and free consultation offers, leading to a significant increase in inquiries and conversions.

Why This eBook?

You might wonder, with so many resources available online, why should you invest your time in this eBook? This eBook is specifically tailored for AI and cloud consulting firms, addressing unique challenges and opportunities in this niche. It provides:

Targeted Strategies: Practical, industry-specific strategies that you can implement immediately.

Expert Insights: Advice and tips from industry leaders who have successfully leveraged social media ads.

Actionable Steps: Step-by-step guides and checklists to help you create, manage, and optimize your ad campaigns.

Comprehensive Coverage: From understanding your market to crafting compelling content and analysing performance, this eBook covers all aspects of social media advertising.

By the end of this eBook, you will have a clear roadmap to doubling your clients and sales using social media ads. So, get ready to dive deep into the world of high-impact marketing and transform your AI and cloud consulting firm into a growth powerhouse.

Chapter 2 Understanding Your Market and Setting Goals

Overview

Welcome to Chapter 2 of "High-Impact Marketing: Growing Your AI and Cloud Consulting Firm." In this chapter, we will delve into the critical steps of understanding your market and setting actionable, measurable goals. By mastering these foundational aspects, you'll be equipped to create highly targeted and effective social media ad campaigns that resonate with your audience and drive meaningful results.

The Importance of Market Analysis

Before diving into ad creation, it's essential to thoroughly understand your market. This involves identifying who your potential clients are, what their needs and pain points are, and how you can address these better than your competitors. Market analysis is the bedrock of any successful marketing strategy, providing the insights needed to tailor your messaging and offerings to meet the specific demands of your audience.

Identifying Your Target Audience

For an AI and cloud consulting firm, your target audience typically includes:

Business Owners and Executives: Individuals making strategic decisions about technology investments.

IT Managers and CTOs: Key decision-makers responsible for implementing AI and cloud solutions.

Industry-Specific Roles: Depending on your niche, this could include healthcare administrators, financial analysts, or retail operations managers.

To identify your target audience, consider the following steps:

Demographic Analysis: Look at age, gender, location, industry, and job roles.

Psychographic Analysis: Understand their interests, values, challenges, and motivations.

Behavioral Analysis: Assess their purchasing behaviour, technology adoption rates, and engagement with digital content.

By creating detailed buyer personas, you can tailor your ad content to speak directly to the needs and concerns of these individuals.

Conducting Competitive Analysis: Understanding your competition is equally important. Analyse the strengths and weaknesses of other AI and cloud consulting firms. Identify gaps in their offerings that you can fill or areas where you can provide superior value. Tools like SWOT analysis (Strengths, Weaknesses, Opportunities, Threats) can be especially useful in this regard.

Defining Your Unique Value Proposition: Your unique value proposition (UVP) sets you apart from the competition. It's a clear statement that explains how your services benefit your clients, what makes you different, and why they should choose you. Your UVP should be at the core of your marketing messages, ensuring that your ads communicate this effectively.

Setting SMART Goals

Once you have a deep understanding of your market, the next step is to set goals for your social media ad campaigns. Goals give your efforts direction and provide benchmarks for measuring success. To be effective, your goals should be SMART:

Specific: Clearly define what you want to achieve. Instead of "Increase sales," aim for "Increase sales by 20% in the next six months."

Measurable: Ensure you can track and measure your progress. This might involve setting up specific metrics like the number of leads generated, conversion rates, or return on ad spend (ROAS).

Achievable: Set realistic goals that are challenging yet attainable. Consider your resources, budget, and the current state of your business.

Relevant: Align your goals with your overall business objectives. If your business goal is to expand into new markets, your ad campaign goal could focus on lead generation in those specific areas.

Time-Bound: Establish a clear timeline for achieving your goals. This helps maintain focus and urgency. For example, "Generate 100 new leads within the next quarter."

Translating Goals into Campaign Strategies

With your SMART goals in place, you can start developing specific strategies to achieve them. If your goal is to increase brand awareness, your strategy might include creating engaging video content that showcases your expertise and client success stories. For lead generation, you might develop a series of ads offering free consultations or downloadable whitepapers in exchange for contact information.

Case Study: Setting Goals for Success

Let's consider the hypothetical example of Tec Cloud Advisors, an AI and cloud consulting firm. They aimed to increase their client base by 30% over the next year. Their market analysis revealed a strong demand for cloud migration services among mid-sized tech companies. By defining a clear UVP around their specialized, seamless migration process and setting SMART goals for lead generation, they crafted targeted ad campaigns. Their goal: "Generate 200 qualified leads in the next six months, with a focus on mid-sized tech firms in urban areas." This clarity allowed them to create highly focused and effective ad content, leading to a significant increase in inquiries and conversions.

Conclusion

Understanding your market and setting SMART goals are the foundational steps for any successful marketing campaign. By knowing your audience deeply, analysing your competition, and defining clear, actionable goals, you can create ad campaigns that are not only effective but also aligned with your broader business objectives. In the next chapter, we'll explore how to craft a compelling ad strategy that brings these insights to life and drives tangible results for your AI and cloud consulting firm.

Chapter 3 Creating an Ad Strategy

Overview

Welcome to Chapter 3 of "High-Impact Marketing: Growing Your AI and Cloud Consulting Firm." In this chapter, we will explore the essential elements of crafting a robust social media ad strategy. With a clear understanding of your market and goals from the previous chapters, you are now ready to dive into the practical aspects of planning and executing effective ad campaigns. This chapter will guide you through setting ad objectives, planning your campaigns, and allocating your budget for maximum impact.

Setting Ad Objectives

Your ad objectives are the foundation of your social media ad strategy. They guide the direction of your campaigns and determine the metrics you will use to measure success. social media offers a variety of ad objectives categorized into three main groups: Awareness, Consideration, and Conversion.

Awareness Objectives

Brand Awareness: Increase recognition and recall of your brand among your target audience. This is ideal if you are new to the market or looking to establish a stronger presence.

Reach: Show your ad to as many people as possible within your target audience. This objective is useful for reaching a broad audience and increasing visibility.

Consideration Objectives

Traffic: Drive users to your website, landing page, or app. This objective is effective for generating interest and directing potential clients to learn more about your services.

Engagement: Encourage interactions such as likes, comments, shares, and event responses. This can help build a community around your brand and increase social proof.

App Installs: Promote your app and increase downloads. While not commonly used in consulting, it's useful if you offer an app as part of your services.

Video Views: Increase the number of views for your video content. Videos are powerful for showcasing your expertise and success stories.

Lead Generation: Collect leads directly within social media through forms. This objective is perfect for capturing contact information and generating potential client lists.

Messages: Encourage users to send you messages on social media Messenger, WhatsApp, or Instagram Direct. This allows for direct interaction and personalized communication.

Conversion Objectives

Conversions: Drive valuable actions on your website, such as signing up for a newsletter, downloading a whitepaper, or requesting a consultation.

Catalogue Sales: Promote products from your catalogue to drive sales. While more relevant for e-commerce, it can be used to showcase service packages.

Store Traffic: Drive foot traffic to your physical locations. Useful if you have a consulting office or host events and workshops.

Choosing the right objective is crucial. For an AI and cloud consulting firm, lead generation, traffic, and conversions are often the most relevant objectives.

Campaign Planning

Once you've set your ad objectives, it's time to plan your campaigns. A well-structured campaign plan ensures that your efforts are organized and aligned with your business goals. Here's how to create an effective campaign plan:

1. Define Your Campaign Theme and Message

Start by defining the central theme and message of your campaign. This should align with your unique value proposition and resonate with your target audience. For instance, if your goal is to promote your cloud migration services, your campaign theme might focus on the benefits of seamless migration and enhanced security.

2. Create a Content Calendar

A content calendar helps you schedule your ads and ensures a consistent flow of content. Plan out the types of ads you will run, the content for each ad, and the dates they will be published. Include a mix of ad formats, such as image ads, video ads, carousel ads, and lead generation forms.

3. Develop Ad Creative

Your ad creative—comprising visuals, ad copy, and call-to-actions (CTAs)—plays a crucial role in capturing attention and driving engagement. Ensure your ad creative is visually appealing, concise, and aligned with your campaign message. Use high-quality images and videos, compelling headlines, and clear CTAs that guide users to take the desired action.

4. Set Up Targeting Parameters

social media's advanced targeting options allow you to reach specific segments of your audience. Use the insights from your market analysis to set up precise targeting parameters. You can target based on demographics, interests, behaviours, and even custom audiences (e.g., existing clients or website visitors). Additionally, lookalike audiences can help you reach new users who resemble your existing clients.

5. Implement A/B Testing

A/B testing involves running multiple versions of your ads to see which performs better. Test different elements such as headlines, ad copy, images, and CTAs. Analyse the results to identify what resonates best with your audience and optimize your ads accordingly.

Budget Allocation

Effective budget allocation ensures that you get the best return on investment (ROI) from your ad spend. Here are some tips for allocating your budget:

1. Start Small and Scale

Begin with a modest budget to test your campaigns. Monitor the performance and gradually increase your budget for the ads that yield the best results.

2. Allocate Based on Objectives

Distribute your budget based on your ad objectives. For example, if lead generation is your primary goal, allocate a larger portion of your budget to lead generation ads.

3. Monitor and adjust

Regularly review your campaign performance and adjust your budget allocation based on the results. Shift more budget to high-performing ads and pause or tweak underperforming ones.

Case Study: Effective Campaign Planning

Imagine Innovate Cloud, an AI and cloud consulting firm, aiming to generate 100 qualified leads in three months. They chose lead generation as their primary ad objective. Their campaign theme focused on the seamless integration of AI solutions in mid-sized businesses. Innovate Cloud created a content calendar featuring weekly video ads highlighting client success stories and monthly carousel ads showcasing their top services. They used social media's targeting options to reach IT managers and CTOs in their target industries and implemented A/B testing to refine their ad creative. By effectively allocating their budget and continuously optimizing their campaigns, Innovate Cloud achieved their lead generation goal ahead of schedule.

Conclusion

Creating a social media ad strategy involves setting clear objectives, planning your campaigns meticulously, and allocating your budget wisely. With these elements in place, you are well-equipped to launch effective ad campaigns that drive growth for your AI and cloud consulting firm. In the next chapter, we'll delve into crafting compelling ad content that captures attention and converts prospects into clients.

Chapter 4 Crafting Compelling Ad Content

Overview

Welcome to Chapter 4 of "High-Impact Marketing: Growing Your AI and Cloud Consulting Firm." Now that you have your market analysis, goals, and strategy in place, it's time to focus on the heart of your social media ad campaigns: the content. Crafting compelling ad content is crucial for capturing attention, engaging your audience, and driving conversions. In this chapter, we will explore different ad formats, tips for creating effective visuals and copy, and the importance of A/B testing to optimize your ad performance.

The Power of Visuals and Copy

In the crowded digital landscape, grabbing your audience's attention within the first few seconds is vital. This is where compelling visuals and persuasive copy come into play. For AI and cloud consulting firms, it's not just about aesthetics; your content needs to convey your expertise and the value of your services effectively.

Ad Formats: Exploring Your Options

social media offers a variety of ad formats, each with its own strengths. Choosing the right format depends on your campaign objectives and the message you want to convey.

Image Ads: Simple yet effective, image ads are great for quick, impactful messages. Use high-quality images that resonate with your target audience. For example, a visually appealing graphic that highlights the benefits of your cloud migration services.

Video Ads: Videos are powerful for storytelling and demonstrating your expertise. Create short, engaging videos that showcase client success stories, explain complex AI solutions, or offer insights into industry trends.

Carousel Ads: This format allows you to showcase multiple images or videos within a single ad. It's perfect for highlighting different aspects of your services or multiple client testimonials.

Slideshow Ads: These are lightweight videos that combine images, text, and sound. They are a good option if you want to create video-like ads without the high production costs.

Collection Ads: Ideal for a mobile-first audience, collection ads offer an immersive experience by combining a cover image or video with several product images. Use this format to showcase your service packages or case studies.

Lead Ads: Designed to capture leads directly on social media, these ads are great for offering free consultations, downloadable whitepapers, or newsletter sign-ups.

Creating Effective Visuals

Your visuals need to be eye-catching and relevant. Here are some tips for creating effective ad visuals:

Use High-Quality Images: Blurry or low-resolution images can turn off potential clients. Invest in professional photography or use high-quality stock images that align with your brand.

Maintain Consistent Branding: Ensure your visuals reflect your brand's colors, fonts, and style. Consistency builds brand recognition and trust.

Incorporate Your UVP: Highlight your unique value proposition in your visuals. For example, use graphics that showcase the seamless integration of your AI solutions or the security features of your cloud services.

Add Text Overlays: Use text overlays to emphasize key messages or benefits. Keep it short and readable, ensuring it complements the image rather than cluttering it.

Crafting Persuasive Ad Copy

Your ad copy needs to be concise, compelling, and aligned with your campaign objectives. Here are some tips for writing effective ad copy:

Grab Attention with a Strong Headline: Your headline should immediately capture interest. Use action-oriented language and highlight the main benefit. For example, "Transform Your Business with Seamless Cloud Migration."

Focus on Benefits, Not Features: While it's important to mention what your services offer, potential clients are more interested in how it will benefit them. Highlight the positive impact, such as increased efficiency, cost savings, or enhanced security.

Include a Clear Call-to-Action (CTA): Guide your audience on what to do next. Whether it's "Sign Up for a Free Consultation" or "Download Our Whitepaper," make your CTA clear and compelling.

Use social Proof: Incorporate testimonials, case studies, or industry accolades to build credibility and trust. Mentioning satisfied clients or notable achievements can significantly boost your ad's persuasiveness.

Keep It Simple: Avoid jargon and complex language. Your copy should be easily understandable and direct.

A/B Testing for Optimization

A/B testing, also known as split testing, is a method of comparing two versions of an ad to determine which one performs better. This is crucial for optimizing your ad content and maximizing ROI.

Test One Element at a Time: To get clear insights, test one element at a time. For example, you can test different headlines, images, or CTAs.

Use social media's Split Testing Tool: social media offers built-in tools for A/B testing, making it easy to compare ad variations and measure performance.

Analyze Results: Monitor the performance metrics of your ads, such as click-through rates (CTR), conversion rates, and engagement. Use these insights to refine your ad content.

Iterate and Improve: Based on the results, make data-driven decisions to improve your ads. Continuous testing and optimization are key to maintaining high-performing campaigns.

Case Study: Compelling Content in Action

Let's take the example of AI Solutions Pro, a fictional AI consulting firm that wanted to increase leads for their predictive analytics service. They decided to use video ads showcasing real-world applications of their service in the retail industry. The video featured a client testimonial from a retail manager who saw a 30% increase in sales using AI Solutions Pro's predictive analytics.

For A/B testing, they created two versions of the video ad: one with a focus on the technical aspects of the service and another emphasizing the business impact. After running the tests, they found that the business impact-focused ad had a 40% higher engagement rate and generated more leads. By refining their message and visuals based on A/B testing results, AI Solutions Pro successfully increased their lead generation and demonstrated the effectiveness of their predictive analytics service.

Conclusion

Crafting compelling ad content is both an art and a science. By choosing the right ad formats, creating eye-catching visuals, writing persuasive copy, and continuously optimizing through A/B testing, you can create social media ads that captivate your audience and drive meaningful results. In the next chapter, we'll explore targeting strategies to ensure your ads reach the right people at the right time, maximizing your chances of converting prospects into clients.

Chapter 5 Targeting the Right Audience

Overview

Welcome to Chapter 5 of "High-Impact Marketing: Growing Your AI and Cloud Consulting Firm." Crafting compelling ad content, as we discussed in the previous chapter, is crucial, but even the best content will fall flat if it doesn't reach the right audience. This chapter will delve into the art and science of audience targeting on social media, a critical component of any successful ad campaign. By the end of this chapter, you'll understand how to identify and reach your ideal clients, optimize your targeting strategies, and leverage social media's powerful tools to maximize your ad performance.

The Importance of Precise Targeting

Effective audience targeting ensures that your ads are seen by the people most likely to engage with them and convert into clients. For an AI and cloud consulting firm, this often means reaching business leaders, IT managers, and decision-makers who are actively seeking the solutions you offer. Precise targeting not only improves your ad's relevance but also enhances your return on investment (ROI) by reducing wasted ad spend.

Audience Segmentation

Audience segmentation involves dividing your broader target market into smaller, more defined groups based on specific criteria. This allows you to tailor your ad content to the unique needs and interests of each segment, increasing the likelihood of engagement and conversion.

Demographic Segmentation

Age and Gender: Identify the age groups and gender most relevant to your services. For instance, decision-makers in the tech industry may predominantly fall within the 30-50 age range.

Location: Target specific geographic areas where your services are in high demand or where you have a strategic interest.

Job Title and Industry: Focus on reaching IT managers, CTOs, business owners, and other relevant roles within industries that benefit from AI and cloud solutions.

Psychographic Segmentation

Interests and Behavior's: Use social media's detailed targeting options to reach users based on their interests and online behaviours. For example, target users who follow tech publications, attend industry events, or show an interest in digital transformation.

Values and Lifestyles: Consider the values and lifestyles of your ideal clients. Are they early adopters of modern technologies? Do they prioritize innovation and efficiency?

Behavioral Segmentation

Engagement Patterns: Target users who have previously engaged with your content or similar content. This can include website visitors, social media page followers, and users who have interacted with your ads.

Purchase Behavior: Focus on users who have shown purchasing intent or behaviour indicative of needing AI and cloud consulting services.

Custom Audiences

Custom audiences are one of social media's most powerful targeting features. They allow you to reach people who already have a relationship with your business, such as past clients, email subscribers, or website visitors. Here is how to create and leverage custom audiences:

Website Custom Audiences

social media Pixel: Install the social media Pixel on your website to track visitors and their actions. You can then create custom audiences based on specific behaviours, such as users who visited your pricing page or downloaded a whitepaper.

Remarketing Campaigns: Use custom audiences for remarketing campaigns to re-engage users who have shown interest but haven't yet converted. Tailor your ads to address their specific interests and encourage them to take the next step.

Customer Lists

Email Lists: Upload your email lists to social media to create custom audiences. This is particularly useful for targeting existing clients with upsell opportunities or promoting new services.

CRM Data: Integrate your CRM data to target users based on their purchase history, engagement level, and other relevant criteria.

Engagement Audiences

social media Engagement: Create custom audiences from users who have engaged with your social media or Instagram content. This includes likes, comments, shares, and video views.

Event Engagement: Target users who have responded to your social media events or interacted with your event pages.

Lookalike Audiences

Lookalike audiences allow you to expand your reach by targeting users who resemble your existing clients or high-value leads. social media uses data from your custom audiences to find new users with similar characteristics and behaviors.

Creating Lookalike Audiences

Source Audience: Choose a high-quality source audience, such as your best clients or most engaged website visitors. The more data you provide, the more accurately social media can create your lookalike audience.

Audience Size: Determine the size of your lookalike audience. Smaller audiences (1% similarity) will be more closely matched to your source audience, while larger audiences (up to 10%) will have a broader reach but may be less precise.

Case Study: Effective Audience Targeting

Consider the example of Cloud Masters, a fictional AI and cloud consulting firm looking to expand its client base in the healthcare sector. They started by creating custom audiences based on their website visitors who viewed pages related to healthcare solutions. Next, they uploaded their CRM data to target existing healthcare clients with new service offerings.

To reach new potential clients, Cloud Masters created lookalike audiences based on their top healthcare clients. They used social media's detailed targeting options to further refine their audience, focusing on healthcare administrators, IT managers, and executives. By running tailored ads that highlighted success stories and case studies relevant to the healthcare industry, Cloud Masters achieved a significant increase in lead generation and client acquisition.

Conclusion

Targeting the right audience is a crucial step in maximizing the effectiveness of your social media ad campaigns. By leveraging social media's advanced targeting options, creating custom and lookalike audiences, and continuously refining your segmentation strategies, you
can ensure that your ads reach the people most likely to benefit from your AI and cloud consulting services. In the next chapter, we'll explore how to leverage social media Pixel and

analytics to track and optimize your ad performance, ensuring you get the best possible results from your campaigns.

Chapter 6 Leveraging social media Pixel and Analytics

Overview

Welcome to Chapter 6 of "High-Impact Marketing: Growing Your AI and Cloud Consulting Firm." In this chapter, we will explore the powerful tools of social media Pixel and analytics. Understanding and utilizing these tools is crucial for tracking your ad performance, gaining insights into user behaviour, and optimizing your campaigns for maximum ROI. By the end of this chapter, you will be equipped with the knowledge to implement and leverage social media Pixel and analytics to transform your advertising strategy.

What is social media Pixel?

The social media Pixel is a piece of code that you place on your website to collect data. This data helps you track conversions from social media ads, optimize ads based on collected data, build targeted audiences for future ads, and retarget people who have already taken some kind of action on your website.

Setting Up social media Pixel

Create Your Pixel:

1. Go to your social media Events Manager.

2. Select 'Pixels' from the menu.

3. Click 'Create a Pixel' and follow the instructions to name your Pixel and enter your website URL.

Install Pixel Code:

1. After creating your Pixel, you'll receive a unique Pixel code.

2. Copy this code and paste it into the header of your website's pages you want to track.

Verify Installation:

1. Use social media's Pixel Helper, a Chrome extension, to ensure your Pixel is correctly installed and tracking events.

Tracking Events with social media Pixel

Events are actions that happen on your website. Examples include page views, purchases, and leads. social media Pixel allows you to track standard events such as:

View Content: When someone views a page.

Search: When someone uses the search function on your website.

AddToCart: When a product is added to a shopping cart.

Initiate Checkout: When someone starts the checkout process.

Purchase: When a purchase is completed.

Lead: When someone submits their contact information.

Custom events can also be created to track specific actions relevant to your business, such as a user downloading a whitepaper or signing up for an online seminar.

Leveraging social media Analytics

social media Analytics offers a comprehensive view of how people interact with your business across devices and platforms. It provides detailed insights into user behaviour, helping you understand how your ads are performing and where you can improve.

Key Metrics to Monitor

Reach and Impressions:

Reach: The number of unique users who saw your ad.

Impressions: The total number of times your ad was displayed.

Click-Through Rate (CTR): The percentage of people who clicked on your ad after seeing it. A high CTR indicates that your ad is relevant and engaging to your audience.

Conversion Rate: The percentage of users who took the desired action (e.g., made a purchase or submitted a lead form) after clicking on your ad. High conversion rates signify effective targeting and compelling ad content.

Cost Per Conversion: The amount you spend to achieve each conversion. Monitoring this metric helps you understand your ad's cost-effectiveness.

Return on Ad Spend (ROAS): The revenue generated from your ads compared to the amount spent. A high ROAS indicates that your ads are profitable.

Creating Custom Audiences with Pixel Data

Using data collected by the social media Pixel, you can create custom audiences to retarget users who have interacted with your website. Examples include:

Website Visitors: Retarget users who visited specific pages or took certain actions.

Cart Abandoners: Reach out to users who added items to their cart but didn't complete the purchase.

Lead Form Abandoners: Engage users who started but didn't complete a lead form.

Lookalike Audiences

Lookalike audiences allow you to find new users who resemble your best existing customers. By using your custom audience as a source, social media identifies users with similar characteristics and behaviours. This can significantly expand your reach to potential clients who are likely to be interested in your services.

Optimizing Ad Performance with Analytics

Analytics provide actionable insights to refine and improve your ad campaigns. Here's how you can leverage these insights:

Identify High-Performing Ads:

Use analytics to identify which ads have the highest CTR, conversion rate, and ROAS. Allocate more budget to these high-performing ads.

Analyze Audience Segments:

Break down performance data by audience segments to understand which groups are most responsive. Tailor your ad content and targeting strategies to these high-engagement segments.

A/B Testing:

Continuously run A/B tests to compare different ad creatives, headlines, CTAs, and audience segments. Use the insights from these tests to optimize your ads for better performance.

Adjust Budget Allocation:

Monitor your ad spend and performance regularly. Shift budget towards campaigns and ad sets that demonstrate strong results and away from underperforming ones.

Case Study: Optimizing with social media Pixel and Analytics

Imagine datasphere Solutions, a fictional AI and cloud consulting firm, aiming to increase their lead generation. They installed social media Pixel on their website to track key events such as page views, lead form submissions, and resource downloads. By analysing the data, they discovered that their blog page visitors had a high engagement rate but a low conversion rate.

To address this, Datasphere Solutions created a custom audience of blog visitors and ran targeted lead generation ads offering a free consultation. They also implemented A/B tests to refine their ad copy and visuals. Through regular monitoring and optimization using social media Analytics, they improved their lead form completion rate by 35% and reduced their cost per lead by 20%.

Conclusion

Leveraging social media Pixel and analytics is essential for tracking, understanding, and optimizing your ad campaigns. By implementing the Pixel, monitoring key metrics, and using analytics to make data-driven decisions, you can enhance your ad performance and achieve your marketing goals. In the next chapter, we will explore budget management and bidding strategies to ensure your campaigns are not only effective but also cost-efficient.

Chapter 7 Budget Management and Bidding Strategies

Introduction

Welcome to Chapter 7 of "High-Impact Marketing: Growing Your AI and Cloud Consulting Firm." In this chapter, we'll delve into the critical aspects of budget management and bidding strategies. Effective budget allocation and bidding tactics are essential for maximizing the performance of your social media ad campaigns while ensuring optimal return on investment (ROI). By the end of this chapter, you'll gain insights into setting budgets, choosing bidding strategies, and optimizing your ad spend for success.

Setting Your Budget

Determining your advertising budget is the first step towards successful campaign management. Your budget should be aligned with your marketing goals, target audience, and overall business objectives. Here are some key considerations when setting your budget:

Define Your Goals:

Clearly outline your campaign objectives, whether it's lead generation, brand awareness, or driving website traffic. Your budget should support these goals.

Consider Your Audience Size:

The size of your target audience influences how much you need to spend to reach them effectively. Larger audiences may require a higher budget to achieve significant reach and engagement.

Evaluate Competition:

Research your competitors' ad spends and presence on social media to gauge the level of investment required to stay competitive in your industry.

Test and Learn:

Start with a modest budget and gradually increase it as you gather data and optimize your campaigns based on performance insights. Testing allows you to identify what works best for your audience without overspending.

Choosing Bidding Strategies

social media offers several bidding strategies to help you optimize your ad delivery and achieve your campaign objectives. The choice of bidding strategy depends on your goals, target audience, and desired outcomes. Here are some common bidding strategies to consider:

Lowest Cost (Auto-bid):

With this strategy, social media automatically bids for your ads to get you the lowest possible cost per result while maximizing your budget. It's suitable for campaigns focused on generating leads, conversions, or website traffic.

Target Cost:

This strategy allows you to set a target cost per result, and social media adjusts your bids to maintain this cost. It's useful for campaigns where you have a specific cost-per-acquisition (CPA) goal.

Bid Cap:

Bid cap allows you to set a maximum bid limit to control how much you're willing to pay for each result. It's beneficial for campaigns with a fixed budget or where you want to prevent overspending.

Cost Cap:

Cost cap enables you to set a maximum average cost per result, and social media optimizes your bids to achieve this target. It's suitable for campaigns where cost efficiency is a priority.

Value Optimization:

This strategy optimizes your ad delivery to maximize the total value generated from your campaign, such as revenue from purchases or leads. It's ideal for e-commerce businesses or campaigns focused on driving high-value actions.

Optimizing Your Ad Spend

Effective budget management doesn't end with setting budgets and choosing bidding strategies. Continuous optimization is essential to ensure that your ad spend delivers the desired results efficiently. Here are some strategies for optimizing your ad spend:

Monitor Performance Metrics:

Regularly track key performance indicators (KPIs) such as CTR, conversion rate, and ROAS to assess the effectiveness of your campaigns. Use these insights to make data-driven decisions and adjust your budget allocation accordingly.

Allocate Budget Based on Performance:

Shift more budget towards campaigns and ad sets that demonstrate strong performance and deliver the best results. Conversely, reduce or pause spending on underperforming campaigns to avoid wasting resources.

Test and Iterate:

Continuously test different ad creatives, audience segments, and bidding strategies to identify what resonates best with your audience. Use A/B testing to compare variations and refine your approach over time.

Implement Ad Scheduling:

Use ad scheduling to control when your ads are shown based on your audience's behaviour and engagement patterns. Focus your budget on peak times when your target audience is most active and likely to convert.

Case Study: Effective Budget Management

Imagine CloudTech Solutions, a fictional AI and cloud consulting firm, wanting to increase their lead generation through social media ads. They started with a modest budget and used the lowest cost bidding strategy to optimize their ad delivery while staying within budget constraints.

By closely monitoring performance metrics and reallocating budget towards high-performing ad sets, CloudTech Solutions achieved a 25% increase in leads while maintaining their target cost per lead. They also experimented with different ad formats and messaging to identify the most effective strategies for engaging their target audience.

Conclusion

Budget management and bidding strategies play a crucial role in the success of your social media ad campaigns. By setting clear goals, choosing the right bidding strategy, and optimizing your ad spend based on performance insights, you can maximize the impact of your advertising efforts and drive meaningful results for your AI and cloud consulting firm. In the next chapter, we'll explore advanced tactics for retargeting and scaling your campaigns to further enhance your marketing strategy.

Chapter 8 Retargeting and Scaling Your Campaigns

Overview

Welcome to Chapter 8 of "High-Impact Marketing: Growing Your AI and Cloud Consulting Firm." In this chapter, we'll explore advanced tactics for retargeting and scaling your campaigns. Retargeting allows you to re-engage users who have previously interacted with your brand, while scaling involves expanding your reach and increasing the impact of your campaigns. By mastering these strategies, you can optimize your advertising efforts and drive further growth for your consulting firm.

The Power of Retargeting

Retargeting, also known as remarketing, is a powerful strategy for reconnecting with users who have shown interest in your services but haven't yet converted. It allows you to deliver personalized ads to these users, reminding them of your offerings and encouraging them to take action. Here are some effective retargeting tactics to consider:

Website Retargeting:

Use social media Pixel to track users who have visited your website but didn't complete a desired action, such as filling out a contact form or making a purchase. Retarget these users with relevant ads to encourage them to return and convert.

Dynamic Product Ads:

Showcase products or services that users have viewed on your website but haven't purchased yet. Dynamic product ads automatically display the most relevant products to each user based on their browsing history, increasing the likelihood of conversion.

Cart Abandonment Recovery:

Target users who added items to their shopping cart but abandoned the checkout process. Remind them of their abandoned items and incentivize them to complete their purchase with special offers or discounts.

Lead Nurturing Sequences:

Create automated email sequences or social media Messenger campaigns to nurture leads who have expressed interest in your services. Provide valuable content, address common questions or concerns, and guide them towards scheduling a consultation or requesting more information.

Scaling Your Campaigns

Scaling your campaigns involves expanding your reach and increasing the impact of your advertising efforts to drive further growth for your consulting firm. Here are some strategies for scaling your campaigns effectively:

Audience Expansion:

Identify additional audience segments that are likely to be interested in your services and expand your targeting criteria accordingly. Use social media's lookalike audiences to reach new users who resemble your existing clients or high-value leads.

Ad Creative Variation:

Experiment with different ad formats, visuals, and messaging to appeal to a broader audience. Test new creative elements and iterate based on performance insights to find what resonates best with your target audience.

Campaign Diversification:

Diversify your ad campaigns across different platforms, channels, and formats to reach users at various touchpoints in their buyer's journey. Consider incorporating video ads, carousel ads, and lead generation campaigns to engage users across different platforms.

Budget Optimization:

Continuously monitor your budget allocation and adjust your spending to focus on high-performing campaigns and audience segments. Increase budget for campaigns that deliver strong results and reallocate resources from underperforming initiatives to maximize ROI.

Case Study: Retargeting and Scaling in Action

Imagine Tec Savvy Solutions, a fictional AI and cloud consulting firm, implementing retargeting and scaling strategies to drive growth. By leveraging website retargeting, Tec Savvy Solutions reached users who visited their website but didn't convert, resulting in a 20% increase in lead generation.

Additionally, Tec Savvy Solutions expanded their audience targeting criteria using lookalike audiences, reaching new users who shared characteristics with their existing clients. By diversifying their ad campaigns across multiple platforms and experimenting with different ad formats, they achieved a 30% increase in brand awareness and expanded their client base.

Conclusion

Retargeting and scaling are essential components of a successful social media advertising strategy for your AI and cloud consulting firm. By re-engaging users who have shown interest in your services and expanding your reach to new audiences, you can drive further growth and achieve your marketing objectives. In the next chapter, we'll explore strategies for measuring and optimizing the overall effectiveness of your campaigns to ensure long-term success.

Chapter 9 Measuring and Optimizing Campaign Effectiveness

Overview

Welcome to Chapter 9 of "High-Impact Marketing: Growing Your AI and Cloud Consulting Firm." In this chapter, we'll dive into the crucial task of measuring and optimizing the effectiveness of your ad campaigns. Tracking key metrics and analysing performance data are essential steps in refining your advertising strategy and maximizing your return on investment (ROI). By mastering the art of measurement and optimization, you can continuously improve your campaigns and drive sustainable growth for your consulting firm.

The Importance of Measurement

Effective measurement allows you to evaluate the success of your social media ad campaigns and identify areas for improvement. By tracking key performance indicators (KPIs) and analysing data insights, you can make informed decisions to optimize your ad strategy and achieve better results. Here are some essential metrics to measure:

Click-Through Rate (CTR):

CTR measures the percentage of people who clicked on your ad after seeing it. A high CTR indicates that your ad is resonating with your audience and driving engagement.

Conversion Rate:

Conversion rate measures the percentage of users who completed a desired action, such as filling out a lead form or making a purchase, after clicking on your ad. A high conversion rate indicates that your ad is effectively driving conversions.

Return on Ad Spend (ROAS):

ROAS measures the revenue generated from your ad campaigns compared to the amount spent on advertising. It helps you understand the profitability of your campaigns and optimize your budget allocation.

Cost per Acquisition (CPA):

CPA measures the cost of acquiring a lead or customer through your ad campaigns. It helps you assess the efficiency of your advertising spend and identify opportunities to reduce costs.

Audience Engagement:

Monitor metrics such as likes, comments, shares, and video views to gauge audience engagement with your ads. Higher engagement indicates that your content is resonating with your target audience.

Strategies for Optimization

Once you've measured the performance of your ad campaigns, the next step is to optimize your strategy based on the insights gained. Optimization involves making data-driven adjustments to improve ad performance and achieve better results. Here are some effective optimization strategies:

Ad Creative Testing:

Continuously test different ad creatives, headlines, and visuals to identify what resonates best with your audience. Use A/B testing to compare variations and optimize your creative elements for maximum impact.

Audience Segmentation:

Segment your audience based on demographics, interests, and behaviours to deliver more personalized and targeted ads. Tailor you're messaging and offers to specific audience segments to improve relevance and engagement.

Bid and Budget Optimization:

Adjust your bidding strategy and budget allocation based on performance data to maximize ROI. Increase bids for high-performing ad sets and reallocate budget from underperforming campaigns to more effective initiatives.

Ad Placement Optimization:

Experiment with different ad placements, such as social media News Feed, Instagram Stories, and Audience Network, to reach users across multiple platforms and devices. Monitor placement performance and adjust your strategy accordingly.

Ad Scheduling:

Use ad scheduling to control when your ads are shown based on your audience's behaviour and engagement patterns. Focus your budget on peak times when your target audience is most active and likely to convert.

Case Study: Optimization in Action

Consider AI Innovations, a fictional AI and cloud consulting firm, looking to optimize their social media ad campaigns. By analysing their performance data, AI Innovations identified that video ads generated higher engagement and conversion rates compared to image ads. They reallocated budget from image ads to video ads and saw a significant improvement in ROI.

Additionally, AI Innovations experimented with different audience segments and messaging to better target decision-makers in their industry. By tailoring their ads to specific audience demographics and interests, they increased click-through rates and conversions, driving overall campaign success.

Conclusion

Measuring and optimizing campaign effectiveness is essential for driving sustainable growth through social media advertising. By tracking key metrics, analysing performance data, and implementing optimization strategies, you can continually refine your ad strategy and achieve better results for your AI and cloud consulting firm. In the next chapter, we'll explore strategies for staying ahead of the competition and adapting to changes in the digital landscape to maintain long-term success.

Chapter 10 Staying Ahead: Adapting to Digital Landscape Changes

Overview

Welcome to the final chapter of "High-Impact Marketing: Growing Your AI and Cloud Consulting Firm." In this chapter, we'll explore the importance of staying ahead of the curve and adapting to changes in the digital landscape. As technology evolves and consumer behaviour shifts, it's crucial for your consulting firm to remain agile and proactive in your marketing approach. By embracing innovation and staying abreast of industry trends, you can maintain a competitive edge and continue driving growth for your business.

Embracing Innovation

Innovation is at the heart of successful marketing strategies. As the digital landscape evolves, new technologies and platforms emerge, presenting exciting opportunities to connect with your audience in innovative ways. Here are some key areas of innovation to explore:

Emerging Technologies:

Stay informed about emerging technologies such as artificial intelligence, augmented reality, and voice search. Explore how these technologies can enhance your marketing efforts and provide unique experiences for your audience.

Interactive Content:

Experiment with interactive content formats such as quizzes, polls, and interactive infographics to engage your audience and encourage active participation. Interactive content is highly shareable and can help increase brand awareness and engagement.

Personalization:

Invest in personalized marketing strategies that tailor content and messaging to individual user preferences and behaviours. Leverage data analytics and machine learning algorithms to deliver hyper-targeted ads and personalized experiences for your audience.

Voice Search Optimization:

With the increasing popularity of voice-enabled devices and virtual assistants, optimize your content for voice search queries. Focus on long-tail keywords and natural language phrases to improve visibility in voice search results.

Adapting to Consumer Behaviour

Consumer behaviour is constantly evolving, driven by changing societal trends, technological advancements, and economic factors. To effectively reach and engage your audience, it's essential to adapt to these shifts and tailor your marketing strategies accordingly. Here are some strategies for adapting to changing consumer behaviour:

Mobile-First Approach:

With the proliferation of smartphones and mobile devices, prioritize mobile-friendly content and ad experiences. Optimize your website and ad creative for mobile viewing to ensure a seamless user experience across devices.

social media Trends:

Stay updated on social media trends and platform updates to align your marketing strategies with evolving user preferences. Experiment with new features, formats, and content types to keep your audience engaged and interested.

E-Commerce Integration:

As online shopping continues to grow, consider integrating e-commerce functionalities into your website and social media channels. Streamline the purchasing process and provide convenient options for users to buy your products or services directly from your ads.

Sustainability and social Responsibility:

Incorporate sustainability and social responsibility initiatives into your marketing efforts to resonate with environmentally conscious consumers. Highlight your firm's commitment to sustainability, ethical practices, and corporate social responsibility in your messaging and campaigns.

Case Study: Adapting to Change

Imagine CloudTech Solutions, a fictional AI and cloud consulting firm, faced with the challenge of adapting to changes in the digital landscape. Recognizing the growing importance
of mobile marketing, CloudTech Solutions revamped their website to be mobile-responsive and optimized their ad creative for mobile viewing. As a result, they saw a significant increase in website traffic and conversions from mobile users.

Additionally, CloudTech Solutions embraced emerging technologies such as artificial intelligence and machine learning to enhance their marketing strategies. They implemented chatbots to provide personalized customer support and used predictive analytics to optimize their ad targeting and messaging. These innovations helped CloudTech Solutions stay ahead of the competition and maintain their position as a leader in the industry.

Conclusion

In today's fast-paced digital environment, staying ahead of the curve is essential for the success of your AI and cloud consulting firm. By embracing innovation, adapting to changing consumer behaviour, and remaining agile in your marketing approach, you can continue driving growth and achieving your business objectives. Remember to stay informed about industry trends, experiment with new strategies, and always prioritize delivering value to your audience. With a proactive mindset and a willingness to evolve, you'll be well-positioned to thrive in the dynamic digital landscape.

Chapter 11 Emerging trends in AI & Cloud marketing

Overview

In the ever-changing world of technology, staying ahead in marketing demands embracing emerging trends. This chapter highlights cutting-edge developments shaping the marketing strategies of AI and cloud businesses.

Key Trends

1. **AI-Driven Personalization**:
   o   Automated audience segmentation using AI tools.
   o   Real-time content delivery tailored to user preferences.
2. **Augmented and Virtual Reality (AR/VR)**:
   o   Immersive demos of cloud solutions using AR/VR.
   o   Use of virtual environments for interactive client engagements.
3. **Generative AI in Marketing**:
   o   Automated ad copy creation and design assistance.
   o   Tools like ChatGPT for engaging customer support.
4. **Predictive Analytics**:
   o   Enhanced decision-making using AI-driven insights.
   o   Understanding market trends before competitors.

Tools to Stay Ahead

- **Adobe Sensei** for design automation.
- **Hootsuite Insights** for real-time campaign performance tracking.
- **IBM Watson** for enhanced predictive analytics.

In the ever-changing world of technology, staying ahead in marketing demands embracing emerging trends. This chapter highlights cutting-edge developments shaping the marketing strategies of AI and cloud businesses.

Key Trends

1. **AI-Driven Personalization**: AI-driven personalization is revolutionizing how businesses engage with their audiences. By analyzing user behavior, preferences, and interactions in real-time, AI tools enable companies to segment their audience with precision. Automated personalization ensures each user receives content, recommendations, or product suggestions tailored to their unique needs. For example, AI-powered platforms can modify website interfaces dynamically for returning visitors or recommend highly relevant content

based on past behavior. This enhances user experience, improves engagement, and significantly boosts conversion rates. Leading tools for personalization include Salesforce Einstein and Dynamic Yield, which empower businesses to seamlessly integrate personalization into their marketing strategies.

2. **Augmented and Virtual Reality (AR/VR)**: AR and VR are no longer confined to entertainment; they are redefining customer engagement in marketing. Companies can create immersive experiences that showcase their products or services in action. For instance, cloud consulting firms can offer VR demonstrations, allowing potential clients to "walk through" their solutions and visualize their impact. Similarly, AR applications can provide interactive overlays, enabling users to explore features or simulate usage scenarios. These technologies captivate audiences, making complex ideas or technical solutions more accessible. By integrating AR/VR, brands can establish themselves as innovative and forward-thinking in their industries.

3. **Generative AI in Marketing**: Generative AI is a game-changer in content creation and customer interaction. From drafting ad copy to designing visual content, tools like ChatGPT, Jasper, and Canva are streamlining creative processes. Businesses can generate highly engaging advertisements, email campaigns, or even personalized customer support responses. For instance, ChatGPT can simulate one-on-one conversations, enhancing user satisfaction with responsive and accurate information. By reducing manual effort and enhancing creativity, generative AI allows marketing teams to focus on strategy and optimization, ensuring they deliver high-quality outputs at scale.

4. **Predictive Analytics**: Predictive analytics leverages historical data and AI algorithms to forecast future trends, customer behaviors, and market demands. For AI and cloud consulting firms, this means better decision-making and more targeted campaigns. By identifying emerging customer needs or predicting market shifts, businesses can proactively position their offerings. Predictive tools like SAS Analytics or Tableau not only assist in designing data-driven strategies but also help identify the most lucrative customer segments. Early adoption of predictive analytics enables firms to stay ahead of competitors and tailor their marketing efforts more effectively.

Tools to Stay Ahead

To effectively incorporate these trends into your marketing arsenal, leveraging advanced tools is essential:

- **Adobe Sensei**: Facilitates automated design creation, saving time while ensuring top-quality visuals.
- **Hootsuite Insights**: Provides real-time analytics, enabling marketers to measure campaign performance and adapt instantly.
- **IBM Watson**: Enhances predictive analytics capabilities, allowing businesses to understand and act on evolving trends.

By utilizing these tools and integrating the above trends, AI and cloud businesses can revolutionize their marketing strategies, ensuring they remain relevant and impactful in a highly competitive market.

Chapter 12 Cybersecurity in Cloud Marketing

Overview

Cloud marketing involves handling sensitive data, which makes cybersecurity crucial. This chapter explores strategies to safeguard your campaigns.

Key Considerations

1. **Data Privacy Regulations**:
   o Ensure compliance with laws like GDPR and CCPA.
   o Provide transparent privacy policies for customers.
2. **Securing Campaign Data**:
   o Encrypt sensitive data, including client details.
   o Use cloud security tools like AWS Shield or Azure Security Center.
3. **Fraud Detection in Ad Campaigns**:
   o Implement AI-driven fraud detection to prevent click fraud.
   o Regularly audit advertising platform logs.
4. **Cybersecurity Best Practices**:
   o Train teams on handling data securely.
   o Monitor campaigns using tools like Splunk or FireEye.

1. The Rise of Cloud Marketing and Associated Risks

1.1. The Shift to Cloud-Based Marketing Tools

The marketing landscape has rapidly evolved from traditional in-house systems to cloud-driven services, enabling companies to manage customer relationships, optimize campaigns, and run analytics more efficiently. Marketing teams now rely on cloud platforms for tasks like:

- **Customer Data Management**: Platforms like **Salesforce Marketing Cloud, HubSpot**, and **Mailchimp** store vast amounts of sensitive personal data that need to be safeguarded from malicious actors.
- **Data Analytics and Reporting**: Cloud platforms facilitate real-time analytics, which provide invaluable insights into customer behavior, but they also make it more challenging to protect large volumes of data.
- **Ad Campaign Management**: Services that handle digital advertising on platforms like Google Ads and Facebook Ads store and process client data continuously, raising security concerns regarding unauthorized access or breaches.

1.2. Cybersecurity Vulnerabilities in Cloud Marketing

While the advantages of cloud marketing solutions are clear, the shift to these platforms comes with inherent cybersecurity risks. These include:

- **Data Breaches**: Personal data, customer behavior patterns, and transaction history stored within marketing platforms are often prime targets for cybercriminals.
- **Account Hijacking**: Attackers may gain unauthorized access to user accounts, allowing them to tamper with advertising campaigns, steal financial data, or post fraudulent content.
- **Insufficient Data Encryption**: If data is not properly encrypted while in transit or at rest in the cloud, it becomes susceptible to being intercepted during storage or transmission.
- **Inadequate User Access Control**: Weak authentication practices, such as poor password hygiene, and failure to implement two-factor authentication (2FA) put systems at risk of unauthorized access.

2. Building a Secure Cloud Marketing Architecture

2.1. Securing Cloud Infrastructure

Before implementing a marketing platform on the cloud, companies should consider the security measures available within the cloud infrastructure to safeguard their data. There are several essential security features and best practices to adopt:

- **Data Encryption**: Encryption must be enabled for both **data at rest** (i.e., stored in databases and storage units) and **data in transit** (i.e., while being transferred between users, marketing teams, and cloud servers). Many cloud providers offer encryption tools, such as **AWS Key Management Service (KMS)**, to safeguard sensitive information.
- **Access Control and Identity Management**: Using **Identity and Access Management (IAM)** protocols, companies can define roles for users based on their level of access and need-to-know basis. Furthermore, integrating **Single Sign-On (SSO)** across all marketing systems can provide centralized access management, enhancing security.
- **Network Security**: Establishing **Virtual Private Clouds (VPCs)** with secure subnets can help isolate critical marketing data and control traffic flow to ensure that marketing data does not mingle with non-marketing data. Also, adopting **firewalls** and **intrusion detection systems** can help spot anomalies in data transfers and network activity.

2.2. Ensuring Data Integrity

When dealing with large-scale marketing data, ensuring its integrity is paramount to the credibility of analysis, campaigns, and reports. Companies must utilize mechanisms such as:

- **Data Integrity Checks**: This includes using cryptographic hashing techniques and checksums to detect any tampering with data and ensuring no unauthorized modifications take place, especially in competitive marketing analytics environments.
- **Automated Backups**: To minimize the effects of cyber incidents or disasters, periodic backups should be conducted automatically, preventing data loss in case of breach or corruption.

- **Logging and Monitoring**: Constant logging of activities within marketing applications allows organizations to detect and track potential malicious activities in real-time, making it easier to diagnose and remediate issues swiftly.

3. Safeguarding Customer Privacy

3.1. Protection of Personal Identifiable Information (PII)

One of the cornerstones of cybersecurity in cloud marketing is safeguarding **Personal Identifiable Information (PII)** of customers. Any misuse or breach of this data can not only damage an organization's reputation but also lead to financial penalties, as per **GDPR** or **CCPA** regulations.
To ensure customer privacy:

- **Data Minimization**: Only collect the minimum amount of customer information necessary to run targeted campaigns. Avoid storing sensitive data such as **Social Security numbers** or **credit card information** in cloud systems unless absolutely essential.
- **Data Anonymization**: In scenarios where vast datasets are being processed for marketing analysis, anonymizing personal details of customers reduces the risk exposure in the event of a breach.

3.2. Regulatory Compliance and Data Governance

Cloud Marketing platforms are bound by various **regulations** around data protection depending on the geographical region, making compliance essential to secure consumer data and avoid regulatory penalties. Some important regulations to be aware of:

- **General Data Protection Regulation (GDPR)**: Applicable to businesses operating in the EU or engaging with EU citizens, this regulation sets strict guidelines around customer consent for data collection, the right to be forgotten, and cross-border data transfers.
- **California Consumer Privacy Act (CCPA)**: For businesses handling data of California residents, the CCPA mandates data protection policies, data access rights, and consumer opt-out capabilities for data sales.
- **Health Insurance Portability and Accountability Act (HIPAA)**: Companies dealing with health-related data must ensure they meet HIPAA guidelines, which include stringent encryption protocols.

Securing **compliance** with these regulatory standards is integral in building trust with consumers, especially in highly regulated industries like healthcare, finance, and e-commerce.

4. Third-party Vendor and Service Provider Risks

In cloud marketing, organizations often rely on third-party service providers for critical functionalities. However, this introduces risks, such as exposure to vendor-related cybersecurity flaws or compliance lapses.

4.1. Evaluating Vendor Security Practices

When choosing a cloud marketing platform or service, organizations should thoroughly assess the vendor's security posture. Questions to address include:

- **Are regular security audits conducted by external entities to ensure the vendor's cloud infrastructure is secure?**
- **Does the vendor support industry standards like ISO/IEC 27001 and SOC 2 for securing cloud operations?**

An organization can request detailed audit reports, vulnerability scans, and certifications from vendors to verify their compliance with high cybersecurity standards.

4.2. Service-Level Agreements (SLAs)

Cloud marketing vendors should include clearly defined security terms within the **Service Level Agreement (SLA)**. These terms may include:
- **Response times for incident handling and breach notification**
- **Uptime guarantees and risk mitigation protocols**
- **Data retention and deletion policies upon contract termination**

5. Best Practices for Securing Cloud Marketing Systems

5.1. Adopt a Zero-Trust Security Model

The **Zero Trust (ZT)** model operates on the principle that no entity—whether inside or outside the network—should be trusted by default. This means constant verification, policy enforcement, and stringent access controls are mandatory throughout the user's interaction with marketing tools.

- **Micro-Segmentation** within cloud environments limits potential threats to only parts of the infrastructure, reducing the overall attack surface.

5.2. Continuous Education and Training

Educating marketing personnel on the **best cybersecurity practices**, including the dangers of **phishing** emails, weak passwords, and suspicious links, is fundamental. Marketing teams should receive periodic training on security protocols to mitigate human errors, which often lead to breaches.

5.3. Incident Response and Recovery Plan

Having an up-to-date **incident response plan** and clear **disaster recovery** strategies ensures that in case of a data breach or security lapse, a swift and efficient response is launched. Regular simulations of these emergency processes enable teams to stay agile and reduce recovery time during actual events.

Conclusion:

Cybersecurity is not just a **technical challenge**, but a **strategic one** in cloud marketing. As more businesses adopt cloud-based marketing tools to optimize their operations, ensuring the **safety of sensitive data** and remaining **compliant** with evolving **global regulations** is vital. By addressing the risks outlined and adopting robust **security architectures**, organizations can strengthen their cloud marketing infrastructures, building trust with consumers and gaining a competitive edge while protecting their brands.

As cloud technology continues to advance and hackers grow more sophisticated, **staying ahead of emerging threats** and investing in security measures will remain critical to protecting marketing data and maintaining business integrity in a competitive digital economy.

Chapter 13 Collaboration Tools for AI & Cloud Team

Overview

Effective teamwork is essential for delivering successful marketing campaigns. This chapter focuses on tools and practices to enhance team collaboration.

As AI (Artificial Intelligence) and Cloud Computing emerge as transformative forces across industries, collaboration among distributed teams has never been more crucial. AI development, cloud infrastructure management, and their integration into scalable applications demand effective coordination, especially given that these disciplines involve a multidisciplinary approach. Teams are required to merge deep technical expertise, from cloud architects to machine learning scientists, software developers, and project managers, making collaboration tools a critical component for success.

This chapter explores the best collaboration tools for AI and Cloud teams, illustrating how they enhance productivity, break down silos, and facilitate seamless cooperation between individuals, teams, and departments. The chapter will cover communication platforms, version control systems, project management tools, and platforms tailored specifically for machine learning workflows.

1. Communication Tools for Distributed AI and Cloud Teams

In AI and cloud-driven projects, maintaining clear communication between team members working in various locations and on complex tasks is critical for success. Effective communication tools are the backbone of teams collaborating in dynamic and ever-changing environments.

1.1. Slack: Real-Time Messaging & Collaboration

Slack has become synonymous with team communication, offering channels for departments, projects, or specific initiatives. In AI and cloud teams, Slack facilitates:

- Real-time discussions: Channels dedicated to specific AI models, cloud infrastructure components, or data science projects allow teams to engage in focused discussions without clogging email inboxes.
- Integration with other tools: Slack integrates with tools like Jupyter Notebooks, Trello, and cloud platforms such as AWS or Azure. This integration is essential as AI teams often work with data and scripts from notebooks or share code via repositories like GitHub.
- Bots and Automation: Slack supports bots (e.g., Jira integration for tracking development tasks) and automated reminders for important deadlines, meetings, or milestones.

1.2. Microsoft Teams: Comprehensive Collaboration Hub

For teams that rely heavily on Microsoft products, Microsoft Teams is a powerful collaboration platform that integrates seamlessly with Office 365, SharePoint, and Azure. It combines chat, file sharing, and meetings within one central platform, which can be pivotal for collaboration across different disciplines within AI and cloud systems.

- Video Meetings and Calls: Built-in video conferencing options ensure cross-team discussions can happen easily, which is essential for brainstorming or resolving deployment issues on cloud services.
- Collaboration on Office Documents: Real-time collaboration on Word, Excel, and PowerPoint documents allows teams to work together on AI and cloud project documentation and system requirements.

2. Version Control for Code and Data Management

AI and cloud projects often involve teams working with large amounts of code, data sets, and machine learning models. Effective version control is necessary to avoid conflicts, facilitate collaboration, and track changes made by individual team members.

2.1. GitHub: Centralized Code Repository

GitHub has been the standard for version control in the software and data science industries. For AI and cloud teams, it provides:

- Collaboration on Code: GitHub allows teams to share code, handle version control, and keep detailed logs of changes. Its branching feature is ideal for AI teams, enabling developers to work in parallel on different algorithms or models without interrupting others' workflows.
- Pull Requests & Code Reviews: Developers can submit their work via pull requests, which can then be reviewed by others for feedback or approval. This ensures quality assurance before pushing machine learning or AI model code into production.
- Integration with CI/CD Pipelines: GitHub Actions and integrations with cloud-based CI/CD tools (e.g., Jenkins, Azure Pipelines) streamline automated testing and deployment. Continuous deployment is critical for managing cloud infrastructure efficiently.

2.2. GitLab: A Complete DevOps Platform

GitLab provides end-to-end functionality that appeals to AI and cloud teams involved in DevOps pipelines. It not only offers version control but also built-in tools for continuous integration, testing, and deployment.

- AI Model Lifecycle Management: GitLab's rich set of tools for version control extends to data versioning and model management, allowing AI and data science teams to manage the development lifecycle of their models seamlessly. It also integrates with MLflow, a popular platform for managing machine learning projects.
- Container Registry: GitLab integrates with Docker and Kubernetes, which is crucial for managing cloud resources and deploying containerized AI applications or microservices to the cloud

3. Project Management & Task Tracking for AI & Cloud Teams

When working on complex AI and cloud projects, team members are often juggling multiple tasks, deadlines, and dependencies. A structured approach to project management keeps teams organized and aligned.

3.1. Jira: Agile Project Management for AI and Cloud

As AI and cloud development projects often follow Agile or Scrum methodologies, Jira serves as an excellent tool for tracking tasks, issues, and progress. This project management software offers:

- Kanban and Scrum Boards: Jira supports project teams in tracking tasks in sprints and agile workflows. For cloud systems or AI models, breaking work into manageable, time-boxed chunks ensures teams are on track to meet deadlines.
- Advanced Reporting: Jira's reporting capabilities provide visibility into sprint progress, roadblocks, and task completion, helping team members focus on priority issues.
- Integration with Other Tools: Jira seamlessly integrates with GitHub for tracking commits and issues, Slack for team communication, and various cloud tools like AWS or GCP for managing the resources needed to support AI models.

3.2. Trello: Lightweight Project Management

While not as feature-rich as Jira, Trello is an intuitive and flexible project management tool that's ideal for smaller teams or individual tasks. It utilizes a card-based approach to visually track project progress.

- Task Management and Visualization: AI and cloud teams can utilize Trello to manage tasks, whether for sprint planning or tracking cloud infrastructure deployment steps.
- Integrations: Trello integrates with various third-party apps (e.g., Slack, GitHub), making it a user-friendly and adaptable choice for teams already embedded in the tech ecosystem.

4. Machine Learning Collaboration and Experiment Tracking Tools

In AI/ML projects, effective collaboration tools go beyond just communicating or managing tasks—they also need to track experiments, manage datasets, and store models in a secure and collaborative manner.

4.1. MLflow: Managing the Machine Learning Lifecycle

MLflow is a powerful platform for tracking machine learning experiments. For AI teams in cloud environments, MLflow allows:

- Experiment Tracking: MLflow's experiment tracking system helps log and compare models, metrics, and hyperparameters. Teams can collaborate by comparing and evaluating different runs to improve performance.

- Model Management: MLflow helps manage models across different cloud environments by storing model artifacts, dependencies, and configurations, essential for cloud-based deployment on Kubernetes or other platforms.

4.2. DVC (Data Version Control): Managing Data in AI Teams

Unlike Git, which handles code, DVC is designed specifically for handling large datasets and machine learning models. For cloud-based teams handling large volumes of training data, DVC facilitates:

- Data Versioning: DVC allows teams to version control datasets, ensuring that each experiment uses the same version of the data, and results are reproducible.
- Collaboration on Data: As datasets become larger and more complex, DVC helps manage data pipelines in an organized and cloud-friendly manner. Integrations with GitHub allow seamless collaboration on data alongside code changes.

5. Cloud-Integrated Collaboration Platforms

5.1. Google Cloud AI Platform: A Cloud-Native Solution

Google Cloud offers a suite of tools specifically tailored for AI and cloud teams. The AI Platform allows for:

- Seamless Collaboration: The platform connects with other Google services such as BigQuery and Google Compute Engine, supporting the entire lifecycle of an AI model. Collaborating teams can easily share datasets, training results, and model predictions.
- Custom Containers: Teams can design, test, and deploy containerized applications in the cloud and integrate them with existing projects without affecting the development pipeline.

5.2. Amazon SageMaker: Streamlined ML Collaboration

AWS SageMaker is another example of a cloud-native tool built for machine learning collaboration. SageMaker facilitates:

- Model Training, Versioning, and Deployment: It simplifies the AI model lifecycle, from data collection to deployment.
- SageMaker Notebooks: These fully managed Jupyter notebooks enable collaborative development, allowing team members to share, execute, and debug machine learning models with ease.

Conclusion

Collaboration tools are a lifeline for AI and cloud teams, fostering communication, tracking progress, managing resources, and ensuring smooth deployment of innovative applications. As teams become increasingly distributed and rely on cloud resources to fuel their AI-driven projects, using the right collaboration tools tailored to these needs is essential for project success.

Leveraging advanced tools like Slack, GitHub, and Jira for team communication and task tracking, alongside platforms like MLflow, DVC, and cloud-native services from Google or AWS, AI and cloud teams can collaborate more effectively. By integrating these tools into their workflows, teams can expedite their innovation, streamline operations, and most importantly, ensure high-quality deliverables.

Chapter 14 Navigating Global Markets

Overview

In the fast-paced, interconnected world of AI and cloud computing, entering global markets offers immense opportunities but comes with unique challenges. Success demands understanding diverse customer needs, adhering to regional regulations, and leveraging technological capabilities that cater to various markets. For organizations leveraging AI and cloud, expanding globally means developing strategies to manage cultural nuances, comply with local requirements, and build solutions that are both scalable and adaptable to different geographies.

This chapter explores how to navigate global markets, focusing on the strategic application of AI and cloud technologies to address regional requirements, optimize operations, and foster growth.

1. Understanding Regional Market Dynamics

Each market has unique cultural preferences that influence how technology solutions are perceived and adopted. Businesses need to:

- Adapt AI models: Incorporate local language support, currency formats, or region-specific features. For instance, sentiment analysis models must be tailored to cultural communication styles.
- Localized Marketing Strategies: AI can analyze regional trends and customer behavior to create personalized marketing campaigns suited to each market's cultural context.

Understanding the economic landscape helps businesses position their AI and cloud offerings appropriately. Leveraging AI for market analysis can reveal:

- Spending habits and purchasing power.
- Demand for specific cloud services or AI solutions tailored to the local economy.
- Competitive landscape insights through data analysis.

2. Compliance and Regulatory Challenges

Expanding to new geographies means navigating a maze of regulations. AI and cloud services are particularly sensitive to compliance issues related to data privacy and usage.
Key regulations such as GDPR (Europe), CCPA (USA), and PDPA (Singapore) impact how data is stored, processed, and transferred.

- Cloud Regional Zones: Deploying cloud infrastructure in geographically appropriate data centers ensures compliance with local laws.
- AI Bias Mitigation: Regulations increasingly emphasize ethical AI practices. Companies must ensure AI models comply with regional fairness and transparency standards.

Organizations must align their cloud services and AI pricing models with local tax codes and import/export laws for software and services.

Technological Challenges and Adaptation

Latency issues, data sovereignty concerns, and lack of local cloud providers can be significant barriers to entry.

- Hybrid Cloud Strategies: Combining public cloud with local edge computing nodes minimizes latency and ensures better compliance with local laws.
- Multi-Cloud Approaches: Using multiple providers like AWS, Azure, and Google Cloud in tandem for different regions ensures availability and flexibility.

To succeed in global markets, businesses need systems that can:

- Scale up or down based on demand across regions.
- Handle language processing for regional dialects and languages.

Leveraging AI for Global Expansion

AI tools play a critical role in navigating global markets, providing actionable insights and automation.

AI-driven tools like predictive analytics and machine learning models help companies analyze new markets effectively by:

- Identifying high-growth regions.
- Segmenting potential customers by preferences, spending patterns, or geographic factors.

In global markets, AI optimizes logistics and supply chains through real-time insights into:
- International shipping patterns.
- Risk management for market entry and inventory distribution.

Building Global Partnerships

Forming strategic alliances with local companies, technology providers, and government bodies can smooth market entry. Local partners can provide:

- Regional expertise to navigate cultural and regulatory challenges.
- On-ground support for deploying AI and cloud services effectively.

To operate globally, businesses must invest in diverse talent pools. Cross-functional and multilingual teams help:

- Address local needs more effectively.
- Enable 24/7 service delivery and problem resolution.

Cloud and AI for Multinational Enterprises

Organizations expanding globally must leverage AI and cloud to achieve uniformity in operations and service delivery while staying adaptable to local variations.

Cloud platforms provide a centralized yet flexible infrastructure for global enterprises:
- Global Reach: Cloud service providers like AWS and Azure offer pre-configured global distribution.
- Localized Customizations: Region-specific configurations allow businesses to adapt global offerings to local needs.

AI systems capable of analyzing diverse data sets empower decision-makers by identifying trends that might vary by region but converge globally, enabling a more cohesive strategy.

Case Studies

An international e-commerce company leveraged AI to deliver localized shopping experiences by analyzing purchasing patterns in each region, boosting sales by 20%.

A software provider adopted a multi-cloud approach to comply with regulations in Europe, Asia, and North America, achieving high service availability globally with reduced latency issues.

Conclusion

Navigating global markets demands a blend of strategic planning, technological adaptability, and cultural sensitivity. AI and cloud technologies are indispensable for achieving these goals, offering unparalleled tools for understanding markets, managing compliance, and building scalable solutions. Organizations that successfully integrate these technologies into their global strategies can not only enter new markets with confidence but also foster sustained growth by meeting the unique needs of diverse regions.

This chapter underscores the critical role of AI and cloud technologies in making informed, adaptive decisions and ensuring seamless operations across global markets. The future belongs to businesses that can innovate while respecting the regional nuances of the customers they serve.

Chapter 15 Future of AI and Cloud growth in Business

Overview

The convergence of Artificial Intelligence (AI) and cloud computing has revolutionized the business landscape, unlocking unprecedented levels of automation, scalability, and innovation. As these technologies continue to evolve, they are poised to become even more integral to the success and competitiveness of enterprises globally. This chapter explores emerging trends, future growth trajectories, and the transformative potential of AI and cloud computing in reshaping businesses across industries.

1. AI-Driven Decision-Making and Process Automation

As AI matures, its role in decision-making and automation will expand, driving more profound changes in business operations.

1.1 Predictive and Prescriptive Analytics

Future AI systems will evolve from merely analyzing past data (predictive) to recommending proactive actions (prescriptive). For businesses, this translates into:
- Improved demand forecasting and inventory management.
- Enhanced customer experience through adaptive personalization.

1.2 Autonomous Operations

AI-powered autonomous systems will dominate industries such as manufacturing, logistics, and finance, enabling:
- Self-healing supply chains that adjust dynamically based on real-time data.
- Fully automated financial systems with risk assessment and fraud detection.

2. Cloud Evolution to Support AI Expansion

The future growth of cloud computing will be intricately tied to advancements in AI, creating a synergistic cycle.

2.1 Edge and Distributed Computing

- The rise of edge computing will complement cloud AI by enabling real-time data processing closer to users, reducing latency.
- Distributed cloud models will provide seamless integration of edge devices into the broader AI ecosystems.

2.2 AI-Native Cloud Services

Cloud providers will offer specialized services for AI, such as pre-built models, AI-as-a-Service (AIaaS), and tailored infrastructures (e.g., GPUs, TPUs) for computationally intensive tasks like deep learning.

3. Industry-Specific Growth Areas

The impact of AI and cloud will continue to deepen across verticals, introducing sector-specific advancements:

3.1 Healthcare

- **AI-Augmented Diagnostics:** AI and cloud platforms will support advanced diagnostic tools powered by deep learning for imaging and genetic analysis.
- **Global Collaboration:** Cloud-hosted healthcare data will drive innovations in personalized medicine and telehealth.

3.2 Finance

- AI-powered algorithms on the cloud will expand into real-time investment analytics and dynamic portfolio management.
- Blockchain technology integrated with cloud AI will redefine transaction security and compliance.

3.3 Retail and E-commerce

- AI will enable hyper-personalized shopping experiences, leveraging cloud to scale across global markets.
- Dynamic pricing and inventory strategies powered by AI will adapt in real-time to consumer demand.

4. Ethics, Privacy, and Compliance

The widespread adoption of AI and cloud in businesses raises ethical concerns and regulatory challenges.

4.1 Responsible AI Implementation

- Businesses will adopt frameworks for ethical AI development, emphasizing transparency, fairness, and accountability.
- AI governance platforms hosted on the cloud will track and audit AI model decisions.

4.2 Enhanced Data Privacy

- Cloud providers will invest in state-of-the-art security protocols, encryption techniques, and data anonymization to meet stringent privacy laws.
- AI-driven security solutions will predict and mitigate cyber threats proactively.

5. Economic Impacts

The growing influence of AI and cloud technologies will shape the future economy, redefining workforce dynamics and global markets.

5.1 Workforce Transformation

- While automation will replace repetitive jobs, it will also create demand for AI architects, data scientists, and cloud engineers.
- Upskilling programs will be essential to prepare employees for AI-cloud ecosystems.

5.2 Democratization of Innovation

- Cloud and AI will lower entry barriers, allowing startups to leverage enterprise-grade tools affordably.
- Platforms offering no-code and low-code AI solutions will empower non-technical users to innovate.

6. Sustainability and Green AI

Sustainability will play a critical role in shaping the future of AI and cloud.

6.1 Energy-Efficient Cloud Infrastructure

- Cloud providers will invest in energy-efficient data centers using renewable energy sources and optimized cooling technologies.

6.2 Eco-Friendly AI Practices

- AI systems will prioritize resource efficiency, adopting techniques like sparsity-based architectures and model pruning to reduce computational overhead.

7. Key Enablers of Future Growth

7.1 Quantum Computing

Quantum computing on the cloud will offer unprecedented computational power for solving complex AI problems, particularly in drug discovery, material science, and cryptography.

7.2 Federated Learning

Future AI systems will adopt federated learning to train models collaboratively across devices without transferring sensitive data, ensuring privacy.

7.3 Enhanced Collaboration Tools

Advanced collaboration platforms will integrate augmented reality (AR), virtual reality (VR), and AI-powered assistants for seamless global teamwork.

8. Case Study: Amazon's Vision for the Future

Amazon continues to lead the AI-cloud revolution, emphasizing innovation in AIaaS (AWS SageMaker), real-time delivery optimization, and personalized recommendations. Their investments in green data centers and AI ethics showcase the future pathways businesses should consider.

Conclusion

AI and cloud computing are no longer just enablers of digital transformation—they are catalysts for shaping the future of business. With advancements in edge computing, quantum systems, and responsible AI practices, their transformative potential will continue to grow. Businesses that proactively embrace these technologies and align them with strategic, ethical, and sustainable objectives will thrive in the evolving global economy.

In this unfolding future, innovation and adaptability will remain paramount, and businesses must continually reassess their AI and cloud strategies to maintain their competitive edge.

About the author

Mangesh Prabhavalkar is a passionate technologist and innovative leader specializing in the intersection of AI, cloud computing, and cutting-edge software engineering. With a deep commitment to solving real-world problems through technology, he thrives on designing scalable architectures and driving transformative digital solutions. His journey has been fueled by a relentless curiosity to explore emerging technologies and their potential to redefine business landscapes.

As a visionary entrepreneur, Mangesh focuses on leveraging technology to create meaningful impact, whether it's through AI-driven systems, modernized applications, or fostering seamless collaboration across teams. He believes in empowering organizations by adopting agile methodologies and harnessing the power of data to unlock new opportunities.

Mangesh's unique approach to technology blends technical acumen with strategic insight, enabling him to seamlessly align innovation with organizational goals. He champions sustainability, ethical AI practices, and inclusive technology solutions to ensure long-term value creation. Beyond his technical expertise, he is an inspiring mentor who fosters a culture of collaboration and creativity.

In every endeavor, Mangesh brings a rare mix of technical depth, strategic vision, and unwavering enthusiasm for shaping the future of technology.